True Hard Facts

K. D. Wood

© 2026 K D Wood Legacy Books

All rights reserved.

For my children, grandchildren and every generation that follows.

Chapter 1 – The Power of Stillness

It may sound strange to start a book about progress by telling you to stop moving — but that's exactly where real growth begins.

We live in a world that glorifies motion. Every second is filled with noise — phones buzzing, emails dinging, schedules crowding out sanity. Somewhere along the way, we started confusing busyness with progress.

True Hard Fact:

Motion isn't the same as movement.

Fact is: You can run in circles all day and never go anywhere. Stillness isn't laziness — it's discipline. It's strength under control. It's the courage to pause, reflect, and choose your next move instead of reacting to everything around you.

The Wisdom of Quiet

Great decisions are almost never made in chaos. Wisdom doesn't shout — it whispers. You'll never hear it if you're always talking, scrolling, or rushing to the next thing.

Stillness gives you clarity. It's the calm water that lets you finally see your reflection. When you slow down long enough to think, you start to hear your own voice again — and sometimes, something deeper beneath it. That's when you begin to separate what's urgent from what's important. What is noise from what is fact.

The Battle Inside

Distraction feels safe because it keeps you from facing yourself. But when you resist that urge — when you sit in the silence long enough to hear what's really going on — something changes. Peace takes root.

You start trusting the quiet. You realize that not every problem needs an immediate answer — some just need space to breathe.

True Hard Fact:

The hardest fight you'll ever face is against your own restlessness.

Your mind will tell you that silence is wasted time. That doing nothing means falling behind. That stillness is weakness. That's a lie.

Stillness Builds Strength

Stillness isn't the absence of action — it's the preparation for it.

It's the pause before the wise response. The breath before the next climb. The silence before understanding.

Even nature proves it. The seed doesn't grow by thrashing; it grows in still soil. The ocean renews itself not in the crashing waves, but in the calm beneath them.

When you master stillness, you build a quiet power that others can feel. Your calm becomes contagious. People begin to trust your steadiness because you're not ruled by chaos.

Be Still — and Know

Every faith, every philosopher, every thinker worth listening to has said some version of the same thing: Be still.

It's not a call to stop — it's an invitation to connect. To listen. To realign. To remember who you are and what truly matters.

When you learn to be still, you stop chasing peace and start carrying it with you. You stop reacting to life and start living it.

True Hard Fact:
Stillness isn't doing nothing — it's doing the right thing at the right time.

Table of Contents

Chapter 1 – The Power of Stillness 1

Chapter 2 — You Are Not the Center of the Universe 3

Chapter 3 — Living from the Inside Out 5

Chapter 4 — Your Thoughts Create Your World 8

Chapter 5 — Your Words Matter 12

Chapter 6 — What You See and Hear 15

Chapter 7 — Eyes That See the Good 18

Chapter 8 — The Company You Keep 21

Chapter 9 — The Power of Now 24

Chapter 10 — Education: The Multiplier Effect 28

Chapter 11 — It's a Matter of Habit 32

Chapter 12 - Energy and Motivation: The Invisible Fuel 35

Chapter 13 — Recognizing Opportunity When It Knocks 39

Chapter 14 — What You Cannot See 44

Chapter 15 — Deciding the Life That You Want 47

Chapter 16 — Don't Wait for the Perfect Time 50

Chapter 17 — Forget About Goals 54

Chapter 18 — When Quitting Looks Easier 57

Chapter 19 — The Strength of Restraint 60

Chapter 20 — Waiting Without Losing Heart 63

Chapter 21 - Standing Firm When Fear Calls Your Name 66

Chapter 22 — The Crossroads of Life 69

A Final Thought… At Least for Now 72

What You Should Know Before We Begin

Fact is: Most people say they want a better life.
They talk about success, happiness, and freedom as if those things are waiting at the end of a straight, well-lit road. But life doesn't hand out rewards for wishful thinking. It tests you. It humbles you. And if you're not grounded in facts, it will break you.

After decades in sales and leadership, I've seen hundreds of people chase success. Some were sharp, ambitious, and full of potential. Yet most of them fell short—not because they lacked talent, but because they lacked facts. They wanted results without reason, rewards without work, and success without sacrifice.

When I began recruiting and training new salespeople across the country, I thought the plan was simple: find good people, teach them proven skills, and help them succeed. But it didn't take long to realize that skills alone don't carry anyone very far. Even the brightest candidates collapsed once the spotlight faded. Without a solid *why*, even the most talented person will eventually lose their way.

That's when I started teaching what I call the **True Hard Facts**—principles born from experience, not theory. They aren't motivational slogans or convenient shortcuts. They're the plain, uncomfortable facts that separate the doers from the dreamers:

- **No one is coming to rescue you.**
- **Success takes longer than you want it to.**
- **Desire fades. Discipline doesn't.**
- **You can't outtalk hard work.**
- **Your "why" determines your "how far."**

These are the facts most people avoid—the ones that don't fit on a poster or sound good in a seminar. But they're the only facts that last.

Over time, I realized these lessons weren't just for salespeople—they were for anyone determined to build a meaningful life. They were facts I wanted my own family to know and live by: my children, my grandchildren, and every generation that follows.

This book grew out of that purpose. It's not filled with quick fixes or hollow motivation. It's filled with facts—the kind that demands you take a hard look in the mirror and then do something about what you see.

If you're ready to stop searching for shortcuts and start building something real, then you're holding the right book.

This is the *best* self-help book you'll ever read—and if you take it seriously, it's the *only* one you'll ever need. – K. D. Wood

Chapter 2 — You Are Not the Center of the Universe
(But You Are Part of Something Remarkable)

Fact is: When we're young, the world really does seem to orbit around us. Every need, every cry, every hunger is answered by someone else's hands. We learn early that if we make noise, the universe responds. No wonder we grow up thinking we're the main character in life's grand story — because for a while, we are.

But life has a way of teaching hard facts. Eventually, the world stops responding on command. You cry, and no one comes running. You work hard and still don't always get what you want. Then you realize something powerful: while your life is precious, it isn't the center of all things. These facts can sting — but it's also one of the most freeing realizations you'll ever have.

True Hard Fact:

The world doesn't revolve around you — but it doesn't work right without you either.

The View from the Mirror

Our minds are wired to see life from the inside out. You've never once seen the world without yourself in it — not from someone else's eyes, not from above. It's why we mistake our perspective for reality. It doesn't make you selfish; it makes you human.

It's the same reason children think that if they close their eyes, you disappear. To them, what they see is what exists. But maturity means outgrowing that illusion.

When you begin to understand that everyone else is also living from the center of their own world — just as real, just as complex, just as meaningful as yours — everything changes. Arrogance turns into empathy. Pride turns into humility. And you start to see life not as a competition for importance, but as a collaboration of purpose.

True Hard Fact:
Seeing yourself clearly starts with seeing others as equals in importance, not extras in your story.

Why We Cling to Center Stage

There's a reason people hold on to the idea that they're the center of the universe: it's comforting. If everything revolves around me, at least I matter. If I'm the main character, then maybe my pain means something — my struggles have purpose, my story has weight.

Fact is: You don't need to be the center to matter. You don't have to control the stage to have purpose.

You are a vital part of something far greater — a single piece in an intricate, living puzzle. Without you, the picture isn't complete. But your piece only fits when you understand where you connect, where you belong, and how you contribute to something bigger than yourself.

True Hard Fact:

You'll never find purpose by standing in the spotlight — only by letting your light help others to see.

From my experience

I've met many people who never learned this lesson. They still live as though the world should arrange itself to suit them. They carry grudges, take offense easily, and feel cheated when life doesn't deliver what they expected.

Don't be one of them.

When you step back — when you stop demanding that everything revolve around you — you finally see the beauty of the whole. You see that life is a dance, not a spotlight. You see how your smallest actions ripple outward and touch people you may never meet.

True Hard Fact:

The universe doesn't owe you attention — but it does offer you a role. Play it well, and you'll find belonging that self-importance can never give you.

Chapter 3 — Living from the Inside Out

The Power of Belief

Fact is: Before anything great is accomplished, it must first be believed possible.

Belief is the seed from which all achievement grows. Without it, even the gifted falter. With it, the ordinary rise to extraordinary heights.

What you believe about yourself, about others, and about life itself sets the limits of your potential. You can't live higher than the ceiling of your own belief.

True Hard Fact:

If you believe small, you'll live small — because no one can outperform their own mind.

The Shaping Force Within

Belief doesn't shout. It whispers — quietly shaping the way you see yourself and the choices you make.

If you believe you're powerless, you'll play it safe, avoid risk, and shrink from opportunity.
If you believe you're capable, you'll act with courage even when the odds are against you.

Belief is not arrogance — it is confidence grounded in fact.
It's not pretending you can do everything; it's knowing that with effort, persistence, and faith, you can do more than you once thought possible.

True Hard Fact:

Belief doesn't make you invincible — it makes you unstoppable.

Where Belief Comes From

Belief doesn't appear out of thin air — it's planted, watered, and shaped over time.
It grows from three main sources:

- **Words.** The voices you listen to either speak possibility or limitation into your heart.
- **Environment.** The culture around you defines what's "normal." Be careful what normal becomes.
- **Experience.** Success, failure, and hardship can strengthen belief or destroy it — depending on what you learn from them.

That's why it matters to feed your mind with facts, surround yourself with people who lift you higher, and treat every setback as a lesson, not a life sentence.

True Hard Fact:

You are always becoming what you believe about yourself.

The Two Lenses of Life

Belief acts like a lens — it determines how you see the world.

Two people can face the same challenge.
One sees failure and stops.
The other sees opportunity and moves forward.

The first never tries.
The second tries and often succeeds — not because of luck, but because belief unlocked motion.

History proves it over and over: the difference between victory and defeat is rarely ability — it's belief.

True Hard Fact:

Your belief shapes your vision, and your vision shapes your reality.

Generational Belief

Your beliefs don't end with you. They ripple outward — through your words, your tone, your example.

Children grow up under the shadow of their parents' beliefs.
A home filled with doubt produces hesitation.
A home filled with faith produces confidence.

When you model belief — belief in perseverance, in purpose, in the power of hard work — you pass strength to generations you may never meet. Your beliefs become your children's blueprint for what's possible.

True Hard Fact:

Change your beliefs, and you change your life — not from the outside in, but from the inside out.

Chapter 4 — Your Thoughts Create Your World

The Architects of Your Life

Fact is: Before anything in your life can change, your thoughts must change.
Every habit, every action, every decision begins in the same place — your mind.

Your thoughts are the architects of your future.
They draw the blueprints, build the foundation, and shape the structure of the life you will live.

Think small, and your life will shrink to match it.
Think fear, and you'll attract failure before you even begin.
But think with courage, faith, and gratitude, and you'll see doors open that once looked sealed shut.

True Hard Fact:

Your thoughts build the house you live in — make sure you like the floor plan.

The mind is the workshop of destiny — what you design there eventually becomes real.

The Voice Inside

Every person carries a voice that never stops speaking.
It's your inner narrator — and it shapes your reality more than anyone around you ever will.

If that voice says, *"You'll fail,"* your mind will make it true.
If it whispers, *"You're not worthy,"* you'll live like you don't deserve success — even when others believe in you.
But when it reminds you, *"You can grow, you can endure, you can win,"* you start to move differently.

Your posture changes.
Your confidence changes.
Your life changes.

True Hard Fact:

The loudest voice in your life is the one in your own head — train it to speak facts, not fear.

Thoughts are invisible — but they show up in every word you speak and every step you take.

The Prison of Negative Thinking

The strongest prison in the world isn't made of bars or walls — it's built of thoughts.

Many people are defeated before the first step.
Not because life was unfair, but because they convinced themselves it was impossible.

They surrender to imagined limits.
They let fear write their future.

But when your thinking changes, your world changes.
Doors appear where walls once stood.
Solutions surface where you once saw only barriers.

True Hard Fact:

You don't live in the world as it is — you live in the world as you think it is.

Your mind can either chain you to mediocrity or free you to build something extraordinary.

Training the Mind

You can't leave your thoughts unguarded.
An undisciplined mind drifts toward fear, doubt, and resentment.

Training your mind begins with awareness.
Pay attention to what you're saying to yourself.
Write it down if you have to.
Then challenge the lies and replace them with truth.

Gratitude is one of the strongest tools you'll ever use.
It doesn't erase hardship — it reframes it.
It turns frustration into focus, pain into perspective, and setbacks into lessons.

True Hard Fact:

You can't control every thought that enters your mind — but you can control which ones you feed.

The Generational Weight of Thought

Your thoughts don't stop with you.
They ripple outward — into your words, your home, and your children.

A mind filled with fear will speak fear into the next generation.
A mind filled with bitterness will pass that bitterness like a family heirloom.
But a mind built on peace, truth, and hope becomes an anchor — one that steadies everyone who comes after you.

True Hard Fact:

Your private thoughts become your public legacy.

You are teaching your family — not just by what you say, but by how you think.
They are learning your patterns long before they understand your words.

Keep This in Mind

What you think becomes what you say.
What you say becomes what you do.
And what you do becomes who you are.

So guard your thoughts as carefully as your wealth.
Direct them with purpose.
Feed them with facts.
Starve the lies before they take root.

Because the world you will live in tomorrow is being built by the thoughts you are thinking today.

True Hard Fact:

Change your thoughts, and you'll change your world — one decision, one belief, one moment at a time.

Chapter 5 — Your Words Matter

Words as Builders—or Destroyers

Fact is: Words are never neutral. They either build or they break.
They can bridge gaps or burn them to ash.
They can lift a person higher than they thought possible — or crush their confidence with one careless remark.

What you say carries more weight than you think. Words linger long after they're spoken.
People may forget what you did, but they'll never forget how your words made them feel.

Your words don't just shape the world around you; they shape the world within you.
The conversations you have with yourself — your *self-talk* — determine whether you rise to challenges or collapse under them.

True Hard Fact:

You can't speak defeat all day and expect victory to show up.

The Voice Within

That quiet voice inside your head is the narrator of your life.
When it whispers *"You can't,"* you hesitate.
When it mutters *"You're not enough,"* you shrink.
When it shouts *"Why even try?"* you stop before you begin.

But when that same voice encourages — *"You're learning," "You're growing," "You've got this"* — it fuels resilience and courage.
Your inner dialogue becomes the script you act out.
Change the script, and you change the story.

True Hard Fact:

The voice you listen to most determines the life you live.

You talk to yourself more than anyone else ever will.
So the question is — are you talking yourself into strength, or into weakness?

Speaking Life into Others

Fact is: Your words can redirect the course of someone else's life.
A teacher's harsh word can silence a student's potential.
A leader's who speaks for justice may awaken courage in thousands.

Think about the times someone spoke belief into you — and how that memory still echoes.
Now remember: you hold that same power every time you open your mouth.

Every conversation adds something — either **weight to someone's shoulders** or **wings to their back.** Choose which kind of person you want to be.

True Hard Fact:

What you say to others becomes the voice they remember when you're not around.

Guarding the Tongue

Fact is: We live in a world that rewards speed — quick comments, instant reactions, hot takes. But wisdom lives in restraint.

Before you speak, ask yourself:

- *Is it necessary?*
- *Is it true?*
- *Is it kind?*

Speak with intention — not just from emotion, but from character.
And when your words wound — because they will, if you're human — apologize quickly. Humility repairs what pride would let die.

"The tongue has no bones, but it is strong enough to break a heart." — *Old Proverb*

Speak carefully. Speak kindly.
Then watch how the landscape of your life — and the lives around you — begins to change.

True Hard Fact:

Your words are seeds. Some grow into weeds; others grow into gardens. What you plant determines the atmosphere you live in.

Chapter 6 — What You See and Hear

Part One: Seeing Through Different Eyes

Fact is: Most people trust their senses without question.
If it sounds true, it must be true.
If it looks right, it must be reality.
That's not wisdom. That's wishful thinking.

Picture this: you leave a tense meeting convinced one person is the problem. The tone felt sharp. The gestures looked impatient. Your memory feels solid—airtight. Then you hear another account. They noticed pauses you missed, context you ignored, intentions you never considered. Suddenly, your "facts" look like fragments.

True Hard Fact:

Your first story is almost always incomplete.

Marcus Aurelius put it plainly:

"Everything we hear is an opinion, not fact. Everything we see is perspective, not the truth."

Hearing isn't understanding. Seeing isn't knowing. Reality exists beyond perception—and wisdom begins when you admit the difference.

A hearing-specific reality check: you replay a voicemail and hear "attitude." Later you learn they were at a noisy gate trying to speak over announcements. Same words, different facts.

Every day, this plays out in simple, dangerous ways:

- A news story, interpreted three different ways by three smart friends.

- A comment one person hears as praise and another hears as criticism.
- A memory you "remember" that conveniently protects your ego or confirms your fear.

Your mind is not a camera; it's an editor. It filters reality through desire, bias, and expectation.

True Hard Fact:

Your brain doesn't show you the world; it shows you your world.

So, what do you do? Pause. Listen first. Observe without labeling. Ask questions that seek understanding, not confirmation. The world won't change—but your experience of it will. Decisions get clearer. Relationships get steadier. The noise drops. Facts gets louder.

Part Two: Lessons in Awareness

Fact is: You will never have the full story—but you can get closer. That's maturity.

True Hard Fact #1 — Hearing ≠ Understanding
Words often carry opinion, fear, or spin. Listen fully; ask, "What else could this mean?"

If you're rehearsing your reply, you're not listening.

True Hard Fact #2 — Seeing ≠ Knowing
Your eyes record perspective, not reality. Don't confuse angle with accuracy.

True Hard Fact #3 — Selective Perception Is Real
You notice what you expect, want, or fear. Look for the detail that contradicts your first impression.

True Hard Fact #4 — Pause Before You React
Speed is the enemy of accuracy. Breathe, get one more perspective, then respond.

True Hard Fact #5 — Curiosity Beats Certainty
Certainty shuts doors. Curiosity opens them—trade "I know" for "Help me see what I'm missing."

Field Guide: How to See and Hear More Clearly (Fast)

- **Name the Story.** "Here's the story I'm telling myself..." then hunt for disconfirming evidence.
- **Triangulate.** One angle is a guess; three angles form a shape.
- **Steelman, Don't Strawman.** Restate their best case fairly; if you can't, you don't get it yet.
- **Separate Said vs. Felt.** Quote the words, then name the feeling—don't mix them.
- **Echo Check (Hearing).** "What I heard you say is ___. Did I get that right?"
- **Strip the Adjectives (Hearing).** Re-state their words with zero tone labels or intent claims.
- **Rewind the Tape.** Notes, messages, recordings—memory is persuasive, not perfect.
- **Slow the Verdict.** High stakes? Buy time: "I'm going to think on this and circle back."

True Hard Fact:

Most conflicts aren't about reality—they're about perspective.
When you slow down and seek more angles, facts come into focus.

Chapter 7 — Eyes That See the Good

The Strength of Gratitude

Fact is: Gratitude costs nothing — but it changes everything.

It doesn't mean life is perfect. It means you stop obsessing over what's missing and start valuing what's already present.

Gratitude doesn't deny pain; it steadies you through it. It keeps your spirit anchored when circumstances shift.

True Hard Fact:

A grateful heart doesn't change your situation — it changes your strength within it.

Shifting the Lens

Two people can face the same problem.
One complains. The other gives thanks.

The difference isn't the size of their burden — it's the focus of their vision.

Gratitude turns scarcity into enough.
It turns frustration into patience.
It turns ordinary days into blessings.

Hardship doesn't disappear, but it becomes lighter when seen through the right lens.

True Hard Fact:

You can't control what you see — but you can control how you see it.

Choosing Gratitude in Hard Places

There will always be reasons to grumble — delays, disappointments, detours.
But there will also always be reasons to give thanks — if your eyes are trained to find them.

I've seen people walk through storms with quiet gratitude. The storm didn't stop, but their spirit never broke. Gratitude doesn't erase pain; it changes how pain is carried.

True Hard Fact:

Gratitude doesn't make life easy — it makes you stronger than what's hard.

The Ripple of a Thankful Life

Gratitude doesn't stay contained — it spreads.
Thankful people are easier to live with, easier to work with, easier to love.

Where bitterness divides, gratitude unites.
Where tension grows, gratitude calms.

When you practice gratitude, you don't just lift your own spirit — you lift the room.
You teach others, by example, how to see the good.

True Hard Fact:

Your attitude is contagious — make gratitude the thing you spread.

Think About This

Gratitude isn't just a feeling. It's a discipline.
It's the daily choice to refuse complaint, envy, and comparison.

If you want unshakable strength — choose gratitude.
If you want peace that endures — train your eyes to see the good, even in small things.

Because once you start noticing what's right, what's wrong loses power.

True Hard Fact:

Peace was never out of reach — you just had to learn to look for it.

Chapter 8 — The Company You Keep

The Influence of Others

Fact is: No one becomes great alone — and no one falls alone either.

The people you surround yourself with will quietly shape the direction of your life more than almost anything else.

Some companions strengthen you. They sharpen your mind, lift your spirit, and challenge you to rise higher. Others drain you. They blur your judgment, weaken your resolve, and pull you down into the same excuses that keep them stuck.

True Hard Fact:

The people you walk with will either push you forward or pull you under — but they will never leave you unchanged.

The Quiet Pull of Associations

We like to believe we're independent thinkers — immune to influence. We're not.

Sit long enough with complainers, and you'll start to complain. Spend time with the dishonest, and small compromises begin to feel natural.

But walk with those who carry wisdom, integrity, and discipline, and you'll find your standards rising without even trying.

True Hard Fact:

You become like the people you're around most — so choose your "most" carefully.

The pull is quiet, but it's powerful.
You rarely feel it day by day — until you look back and realize you've drifted.

Two Kinds of People

There are really only two kinds of companions in life: those who **add** and those who **subtract.**

The ones who add leave you better than they found you.
Their presence strengthens your confidence, calms your chaos, and calls you higher.

The ones who subtract do the opposite.
They drain your energy, stir resentment, or lure you into compromise.

True Hard Fact:

Everyone in your life is either a ladder or a weight. Know which one you're holding onto.

You can't always avoid negativity, but you can refuse to make it your home.

Guarding Your Circle

Not everyone deserves equal access to your life.
Love all people — but not all people should have a voice in your decisions.

Seek out friends who are honest when truth is hard, loyal when loyalty costs something, and steady when life shakes.
When you find someone whose life reflects the kind of character you want for yourself — keep that person close.

At the same time, have the courage to set boundaries.
If someone poisons your peace, mocks your growth, or constantly pulls you down, you cannot afford to keep them close.

True Hard Fact:

You can forgive someone without giving them access.

Guard your circle like you would guard your home — because what enters your circle eventually enters your heart.

The circle you choose today will ripple outward for years — influencing not just your future, but theirs. Show me your closest circle, and I can tell you where your life is heading.

Keep This in Mind

You are free to choose your companions.
But you are never free from their influence.

That influence is shaping you even now — sharpening or dulling, building or breaking.

The company you keep is the clearest reflection of who you are — and a preview of who you're becoming.
So choose wisely.
Because no one walks alone for long without starting to walk alike.

True Hard Fact:

The voices you let around your table will echo in your children's lives long after you're gone.

Chapter 9 — The Power of Now

Living Everywhere but Here

Fact is: Most people spend their lives everywhere except where they actually are.

Their minds sprint into the future — worrying, planning, and predicting.
Then they drift backward — replaying mistakes, reliving regrets, rewriting what can't be changed.

Meanwhile, the only thing that truly belongs to them — *the moment they're in* — quietly slips away.

Think about it. Every experience you've ever had happened in one place: **now.**
The past is memory. The future is imagination. The present is the only place that's real.

True Hard Fact:

If you can't live now, you can't live at all — because now is all you ever have.

Why the Present Matters

Living in the present doesn't mean ignoring your dreams or forgetting your lessons.
It means refusing to let either one steal the life you could be living today.

- **Joy deepens:** Ordinary moments become extraordinary when you actually notice them.
- **Stress lessens:** You stop drowning in *what if* and deal with *what is*.

- **Relationships strengthen:** People feel seen when you give them your full attention.
- **Clarity grows:** The present reveals answers the future can't yet show you.

Every moment carries power — the power to choose, to love, to change, to build.
Tomorrow is shaped by the choices you make today, and yesterday can't be edited.

True Hard Fact:

The only place you can change your life is the place you're standing right now.

Practicing Presence

Being present isn't about perfection — it's about attention.
It's choosing awareness over autopilot.

It looks like:

- Listening instead of waiting for your turn to talk.
- Tasting your meal instead of scrolling through your phone.
- Noticing the sound of laughter, the warmth of sunlight, the quiet between moments.

Presence isn't a technique — it's a decision to *show up* for your own life.

True Hard Fact:

Distraction is the enemy of peace. Attention is the path to it.

The Cost of Distraction

We live in a world built to steal your focus. Notifications, noise, endless scrolling — all designed to make you react instead of reflect.

The result? You end up everywhere at once and nowhere at all. Always busy, rarely present. Always connected, seldom alive.

Technology isn't the enemy — unconsciousness is.
When you let the world dictate your attention, you trade the richness of real life for the illusion of urgency.

True Hard Fact:

If you don't control your attention, someone else will.

Anchoring Yourself to the Moment

The most powerful people you'll ever meet share one trait: they know how to *pause*.
Before they speak, they breathe. Before they decide, they observe. Before they react, they think.

That pause is presence — the gap where wisdom lives.

Try this:
When you feel overwhelmed, stop and take one slow breath.
When you're angry, wait before responding.
When you're bored, look around instead of reaching for a distraction.

Each time you do, you train your mind to return home — to the present.

True Hard Fact:

Peace doesn't come from escaping life — it comes from engaging it fully.

A Final Fact

This moment — this breath, this heartbeat — is your life.
Not the one you plan to start tomorrow. Not the one you lost yesterday.

This one.

So, pause. Look around. Feel it.
This is where life happens.
Don't rush past it. Don't wish it away.

Because someday you'll realize the *small moments* were the *big ones*.

True Hard Fact:

Yesterday is gone. Tomorrow isn't promised. But now — now is yours. Use it well.

Chapter 10 — Education: The Multiplier Effect

More Than Schooling

Fact is: Education is more than degrees, diplomas, or classrooms. It's not about sitting in a chair and passing a test. It's about staying curious, building wisdom, and growing stronger with each new lesson life brings.

Real education doesn't end when you walk out of school — it begins the moment you realize how much you still don't know.
It multiplies your opportunities — not just in the money you earn, but in the *confidence* you project, the *creativity* you express, and the *contribution* you make.

"An investment in knowledge pays the best interest." — *Benjamin Franklin*

True Hard Fact:

A diploma can open a door, but only curiosity will keep it open.

Why Education Multiplies Value

Unlike possessions, education can't be stolen or worn out. It compounds like interest — the more you use it, the more it grows.

Every new skill connects to the ones before it, multiplying your capacity to think, create, and lead. Education doesn't just *add* to your life — it *multiplies* it.

- **Financial Impact:** Education increases earning potential, but more importantly, it improves your judgment about money, risk, and opportunity.
- **Personal Impact:** It sharpens your thinking, broadens perspective, and helps you see patterns others miss.

- **Social Impact:** It equips you to teach, mentor, and inspire — to lift others as you climb.

True Hard Fact:

Knowledge earns interest every day you put it to work.

Education doesn't just open doors — it teaches you which doors are worth walking through.

Beyond Formal Schooling

Formal education is one path — but it's not the only one.
Some of the world's most influential thinkers and builders didn't just collect diplomas; they collected experiences.

Thomas Edison had three months of formal schooling.
Steve Jobs dropped out of college — but never stopped learning.
Oprah Winfrey built an empire by turning lessons from hardship into wisdom for millions.

Their stories prove the point: the best education doesn't come with a certificate; it comes with *commitment*.

- Books expand your thinking.
- Conversations stretch your perspective.
- Mistakes teach what success never will.
- Experience becomes the greatest classroom you'll ever sit in.

True Hard Fact:

The world itself is a classroom — but only for those humble enough to keep learning.

Barriers and Breakthroughs

Many people stop learning not because they can't — but because they won't.
They let fear, pride, or excuses become their teachers instead.

"I'm too old."
"I don't have time."
"It's too expensive."

Those are not barriers. Those are beliefs.

Education today is more accessible than ever — through libraries, online courses, podcasts, mentors, and free resources that didn't exist a generation ago.
The real barrier isn't access — it's **commitment**.

True Hard Fact:

If you can't invest money, invest time. If you can't invest time, invest effort. Excuses don't educate — effort does.

Applied Learning — Turning Knowledge into Power

Learning without application is like gathering tools and never building anything.
The real power of education isn't what you *know* — it's what you *do* with what you know.

Every lesson should turn into action:

- A new idea applied at work.
- A better way to manage your money.
- A wiser approach to conflict, parenting, or faith.

When you practice what you learn, knowledge turns into wisdom — and wisdom turns into results.

True Hard Fact:

Information fills your head. Application fills your life.

Lifelong Learning — The Edge That Never Dulls

The world is changing faster than ever. Technology, markets, and industries evolve daily. The only true security you'll ever have is your ability to keep learning, adapting, and improving.

Stay curious. Keep reading. Ask questions.
Find mentors. Teach others.
And most importantly — never believe you've "arrived."

The moment you stop learning, you start falling behind.
But the moment you recommit to growth, you become unstoppable.

True Hard Fact:

Education multiplies everything it touches—your opportunities, your confidence, and your ability to impact others. Commit to being a lifelong learner, and your life will continue to expand.

Chapter 11 — It's a Matter of Habit

The Quiet Builders of Character

Fact is: Dreams may set direction, but habits decide destination.

You don't rise to the level of your goals — you fall to the level of your habits.
What you do repeatedly, often without thinking, is shaping the person you're becoming.

Habits are the hidden roots of your life. You don't see them growing, but they decide whether you stand strong or collapse in the storm.

True Hard Fact:

Your habits are building your future — whether you're paying attention or not.

Why Habits Matter

Think of a stone staircase. Each step feels small, but together they carry you higher.
Habits are those steps. You may not feel the progress every day, but years later you'll be standing exactly where your habits led you.

Good habits are quiet builders. They don't announce themselves, but they pay dividends in peace, strength, and stability.
Bad habits are quiet destroyers. They whisper, *"Just this once won't matter,"* until your direction changes by inches — and those inches become miles.

True Hard Fact:

Repetition, not intention, decides results.

The Two Roads of Habit

Life gives you two roads: discipline or neglect.

On the **road of neglect**, days slip by unnoticed. Laziness feels comfortable. Excuses sound reasonable. Small compromises pile up until they bury your potential.
That road always ends in regret.

On the **road of discipline**, the steps are harder — early mornings, tough choices, delayed gratification. But that road ends in freedom, respect, and peace.

True Hard Fact:

Discipline is painful for a moment. Regret is painful for a lifetime.

Habits are the difference between the two. They don't care what you intend — only what you repeat.

Habits Across the Seasons of Life

When you're **young**, habits build your foundation. They teach you self-control and set your compass.
In the **middle years**, habits keep you steady. They hold you when life gets heavy and decisions grow complex.
In your **later years**, habits become your legacy. They no longer require thought — they are who you are.

Your family will remember the rhythm of your habits more than the words of your advice.
They will live with the atmosphere you created: consistency or chaos, patience or pressure, gratitude or complaint.

True Hard Fact:

Your children may forget your speeches — but they will never forget your patterns.

Building Strong Habits

Lasting habits don't start with big promises; they start with small faithfulness.

Pick one thing that matters. Do it daily.
Replace what's harmful with what's helpful. Nature hates a vacuum — if you remove a bad habit, fill the space before the old one returns.

Accountability matters. When someone you trust walks with you, your resolve doubles.

And remember: habits aren't proven on easy days. They're proven when it would be easier to quit — but you don't. That's when roots grow deep.

True Hard Fact:

Consistency beats intensity — every time.

The Final Measure

The life you'll live ten, twenty, thirty years from now is being built by the habits you're practicing today ask yourself: Are the habits you keep right now quietly building the life you want? Or are they leading you toward a future you'll wish you could undo?

True Hard Fact:

Your habits are the prophecy of your future — and you're writing it every day.

Chapter 12 - Energy and Motivation: The Invisible Fuel

Motivation Alone Isn't Enough

Fact is: Motivation is unreliable.
It flares up when things are exciting, then disappears the moment things get hard.

People say, *"I just need to find my motivation."*
But motivation isn't something you find — it's something you feed.

Motivation is a spark.
Energy is the fuel.
Without energy, even the strongest spark burns out before the fire starts.

True Hard Fact:

You can't run on passion alone. Fire needs fuel, and drive needs energy.

Understanding the Difference

Motivation and energy are partners, but they play different roles.
Knowing the difference can change how you approach every dream.

- **Motivation is your "why."** It's the vision that pulls you forward — your cause, your dream, your reason.
- **Energy is your "how."** It's the strength — physical, mental, emotional — to act on that reason.

Think of motivation as the ignition.
Energy is the gas in the tank.
One without the other leaves you stalled.
Together, they create momentum.

True Hard Fact:

A powerful "why" without energy is a dream. Energy without purpose is noise. You need both to move.

The Feedback Loop

Motivation and energy don't live in separate worlds. They feed each other in a loop — either upward or downward.

- **Energy fuels motivation.** When you're rested, nourished, and moving your body, your dreams feel reachable. When you're exhausted, even small tasks feel impossible.
- **Motivation directs energy.** Purpose gives your effort direction. Without it, you waste energy on distractions that don't matter.
- **Momentum multiplies both.** Small wins build belief. Belief drives motivation. Motivation fuels energy. The cycle grows stronger with every step you take.

True Hard Fact:

The best way to get motivated is to do something — not wait for something.

How to Harness Both

If you want lasting drive, build it. Don't wait for it.

1. **Clarify Your Why.**
   Write down why your dreams matter. Not the surface reason — the real one.
   The deeper your why, the longer your motivation lasts.

   True Hard Fact: *A shallow reason quits early. A deep reason fights to the end.*

2. **Protect Your Energy.**
   Sleep, hydration, movement, and nutrition aren't luxuries — they're non-negotiables.
   When your body breaks down, your ambition follows.

   True Hard Fact: *Your body isn't just your vehicle — it's your engine. Treat it like one.*

3. **Create Micro-Momentum.**
   Start small. Do one meaningful thing — finish it — then let that win fuel the next.
   Success creates energy. Energy creates consistency.

   True Hard Fact: *Small wins stacked daily build unstoppable force.*

4. **Guard Your Fuel.**
   Energy leaks through distractions, negativity, and noise.
   Protect your attention like money — because it's worth even more.

   True Hard Fact: *Where your attention goes, your energy flows.*

5. **Schedule for Peak Energy.**
   Notice when you feel most alert — morning, evening, midday — and plan your most important tasks for that window. Don't fight your rhythm. Use it.

   True Hard Fact: *You can't create more hours — but you can create more power in the hours you have.*

The Real Source of Drive

People who seem endlessly motivated aren't superhuman — they're strategic.
They build systems that protect their energy and reinforce their purpose.

They don't wait to feel inspired; they act, and inspiration follows.
They don't chase motivation; they create momentum.

True Hard Fact:

Motivation is emotional. Energy is intentional. Build both, and your drive becomes unstoppable.

The Bottom Line

Motivation gives you direction.
Energy gives you power.
When they align, momentum takes over — and small steps become unstoppable progress.

So take care of your body. Guard your focus. Protect your "why."

Because once you master energy and motivation, you stop chasing drive — and start living it.

True Hard Fact:

The world doesn't belong to the motivated — it belongs to the energized.

Chapter 13 — Recognizing Opportunity When It Knocks

The Quiet Arrival of Opportunity

Fact is: Opportunity rarely announces itself with fanfare.
It doesn't show up wearing a name tag or a flashing sign that says *"This is your big break."*

It usually arrives quietly — disguised as risk, uncertainty, or even inconvenience.
It looks like hard work, a long shot, or something that might not pay off.

The question isn't whether opportunity exists. It always does.
The real question is whether you'll **recognize it, trust it, and act on it** before it passes you by.

True Hard Fact:

Opportunity doesn't shout — it whispers. You have to be still enough, and brave enough, to hear it.

What It Looks Like in Real Life

Consider this:

- **1970:** Walmart went public at $16.50 a share.
  With multiple splits over the decades, that one share would now be 2,048 shares — worth nearly **$287,000 today**.
- **March 1986:** Microsoft launched its IPO at $21 a share.
  If you had purchased just one share that day, through nine stock splits that single share would now be 288 shares — worth roughly **$141,000 today**, not counting dividends.

Those numbers aren't just about money — they're about *vision*.
Someone saw potential in an unproven company. Someone took a calculated risk while most people looked the other way.

True Hard Fact:

What looks small today can become monumental tomorrow — if you have the courage to act while others hesitate.

The lesson isn't about stocks. It's about perception — about seeing *value* where others only see uncertainty.

Most people in 1970 couldn't imagine the empire Walmart would build.

Most people in 1986 had no clue what Microsoft would become.

But a few people did. They looked beyond the surface, and they believed in possibility.

The Nature of Opportunity

Opportunity doesn't always look glamorous.
It often shows up wearing work clothes.

It can be an unpolished idea.
A struggling startup.
A side project no one else takes seriously.
An invitation to try something new that feels uncomfortable.

Real opportunities come wrapped in **risk** — and require **faith**.
They ask for your time, your attention, and sometimes your pride.

But here's the payoff: when you learn to recognize those small, quiet chances and take them seriously, they can change everything.

True Hard Fact:

You'll never find opportunity if you're only looking for comfort.

The Opportunity Mindset

Opportunities aren't rare. They're everywhere. Most people just don't recognize them.
To change that, you have to retrain your vision — to start seeing *potential* instead of just *problems*.

Here's how:

- **Stay Curious** — Ask, *"What could this become?"* instead of *"What is this right now?"*
- **Look for Patterns** — Listen for repeated needs, frustrations, or gaps. Where others see complaints, you should see possibility.
- **Trust Your Instincts** — If something keeps tugging at your attention, there's a reason. Don't ignore it.
- **Act with Courage** — Opportunities expire. Fear delays action. Hesitation is the graveyard of good ideas.

True Hard Fact:

You don't have to be the smartest person in the room to succeed — just the one willing to move first.

Barriers to Recognition

If opportunity is everywhere, why do so few people seize it?

Because it doesn't look the way they expect.
They wait for certainty — and miss their moment.
They want guarantees — and let fear talk them out of motion.

The truth is, opportunity often shows up **in disguise**:

- As a job that teaches you what not to do.
- As a setback that forces you to build new skills.
- As a problem that no one else has the patience to solve.

True Hard Fact:

Opportunity rarely feels like opportunity when it begins. It feels like work.

Acting Before the Window Closes

Opportunities don't last forever. They have an expiration date — and no renewal notice.
If you wait for perfect timing, you'll miss it every time.

That's why decisive people often seem "lucky."
They're not luckier — they're just quicker to act.

They trust that motion creates momentum, and momentum creates results.
You don't need to be reckless — but you do need to be ready.

When something stirs your interest, start small, start cautious — but **start.**

True Hard Fact:

You can recover from a wrong decision. You can't recover from never deciding at all.

Developing Vision for the Long Game

Fact is: Every opportunity demands patience.
Walmart and Microsoft didn't become empires overnight — they grew because people *held on* when others cashed out.

It's easy to chase shiny, short-term wins. But the biggest rewards come to those who recognize long-term potential and have the discipline to wait.

Vision isn't guessing what's next — it's committing to what's worthwhile.

True Hard Fact:

Most people miss fortune because they were looking for fireworks instead of foundations.

Final Perspective: The Knock You Don't Want to Miss

You won't catch every opportunity. No one does.
But if you train your eyes to see potential where others see problems, you'll find more open doors than you ever imagined.

Remember this:
Great opportunities rarely *look* great in the beginning.
They look ordinary. Uncertain. Even uncomfortable.
But when you learn to recognize and act on them, you plant seeds that can grow into something extraordinary.

True Hard Fact:

Opportunity doesn't belong to the lucky — it belongs to the ready.

Chapter 14 — What You Cannot See

The Anchor of Faith

Fact is: There will be seasons when life feels uncertain — when answers hide, and the path ahead goes dim.

In those moments, faith becomes the anchor that holds you steady.

Faith is trust — trust that there's a purpose beyond what you can see, that your steps matter, and that the unseen is just as real as the visible.

Without faith, life becomes a gamble.
With faith, even hardship takes on meaning.

True Hard Fact:

Faith doesn't remove the storm — it keeps you anchored through it.

Strength Beyond Yourself

Faith reminds you of something most people forget: you're not the center of the universe — and you don't have to carry its weight.

It teaches humility. It reminds you that your strength, no matter how great, will eventually run out.

The person who leans on faith will stand when everything else falls apart.

Faith doesn't make life easy — it makes you unbreakable.

True Hard Fact:

When your strength ends, faith begins.

When Faith Is Tested

It's easy to speak of faith when life is comfortable. But real faith isn't proven in calm waters — it's proven in the storm.

Tests don't destroy faith; they refine it.
Just as fire strengthens steel, adversity strengthens belief.

Without testing, faith stays fragile. With testing, it becomes solid and unshakable.

True Hard Fact:

Faith untested is opinion. Faith proven is power.

Living by Faith, Not by Sight

Much of what matters in life can't be measured.
You can't see love, yet you know it by its fruit.
You can't touch hope, yet it keeps you moving forward.
Faith is the same — unseen, but undeniable.

Living only by sight will leave you anxious, because sight is limited. Living by faith lets you move forward even when the outcome is hidden.

Faith teaches trust in the process, not the illusion of control.

True Hard Fact:

You'll never have all the answers — but you can always take the next step.

Faith in Daily Life

Faith isn't confined to sacred spaces. It shows up in how you speak, work, and respond when life tests you.

- **Faith steadies your words** — helping you speak hope instead of despair.
- **Faith shapes your work** — teaching you to act with integrity, even when no one's watching.
- **Faith calms your fears** — reminding you that unseen strength outweighs visible obstacles.

Faith is not meant to stay private. It's meant to be lived — quietly, consistently, and courageously.

True Hard Fact:

Faith isn't something you hold — it's something that holds you.

The Fruit of Faith

When lived out, faith produces qualities that can't be faked.

- **Faith produces courage,** because you believe the unseen is stronger than the obstacle.
- **Faith produces peace,** because you trust that your future is secure.
- **Faith produces endurance,** because you know your labor is not in vain.

And when faith grows in you, it spills over to others.
Your calm steadies them.
Your example strengthens them.
Your life becomes a living testimony that unseen things are often the most real of all.

True Hard Fact:

The strongest evidence of faith isn't what you say — it's how you live when everything is uncertain.

Chapter 15 — Deciding the Life That You Want

Begin with Clarity

Fact is: You can't build the life you want until you decide what that life looks like. If you don't decide the life you want, life will give you what it will – and that might be far from what you want. Without clarity, you drift. With clarity, you build.

For some, the dream is wealth. For others, peace. Some crave recognition; others crave freedom. There is no wrong desire — only undefined direction.

Be careful, though, when you measure your dreams against someone else's life. You don't know what it cost them. What you envy may have been bought with time, peace, or integrity.

True Hard Fact:

You can have almost anything you want — but you can't have everything. Choose what matters most, then pay the price willingly.

Clarity is power. Once you decide what you want, every choice becomes easier — because every decision either moves you closer or farther from it.

The Urgency of Beginning

If you want the life you envision, **start now.**

The days may feel long, but the years are short. Procrastination steals quietly. One day you look up and realize you traded your dreams for comfort, and your time for excuses.

True Hard Fact:

You'll never be ready — you'll just be late if you wait.

Don't explain your ambitions to everyone. Most people don't care unless it affects their own lives. Worse, they'll offer opinions dressed as advice. They'll question your vision, your timing, even your sanity — not because they see clearer, but because they don't see what you see.

Not every dream needs to be shared before it takes root.

True Hard Fact:

Vision grows best in silence.

Walking Your Own Path

No one else can tell you what life you should live.
They can guess, advise, and project — but only you know the voice that calls you forward.

Even those closest to you — friends, mentors, even your spouse — will not always understand. Not because they don't love you, but because they're not you.

Life is personal. Purpose is personal.
Don't hand the steering wheel of your life to anyone else.

True Hard Fact:

You can't follow your calling while chasing approval.

Walking your own path means accepting solitude when necessary. The crowd may not understand your direction — but that's fine. Great lives are rarely lived in the middle of the herd.

Guardrails for Living Well

If you want to build a strong life, you need strong principles.
These aren't restrictions — they're protection.

- **Don't expect others to support you.** Help may come, but it should never be the condition for your progress.
- **Never expect more from others than you demand from yourself.** Responsibility is personal.
- **Earn what you receive.** What's unearned is rarely valued, and what's earned builds strength.

True Hard Fact:

Character isn't formed by what you get — it's forged by what you're willing to earn.

The Final Measure

A life worth living is one worth dying for.
That's the ultimate test.

If what you're pursuing isn't worth your time, your energy, and your heart — it's not worth your life.

So decide.
Then begin.
Then build.

Don't drift. Don't delay.
Make your days count for something that will still matter when you're gone.
When the end comes, may you look back and say: **"Yes — it was worth it."**

True Hard Fact:

The life you want won't happen by chance — it happens by choice.

Chapter 16 — Don't Wait for the Perfect Time

The Lie of the "Right Moment"

One of the most dangerous lies you'll ever believe is this: *"I'll start when the time is right."*

Fact is: We tell ourselves we're waiting for the perfect moment — when fear is smaller, money is available, the plan is flawless, or the timing feels ideal.
But that moment never comes.

Life is never neat. Conditions are never perfect. The "right time" is a myth that keeps you standing still.

True Hard Fact:

If you wait for perfect, you'll wait forever.

The Weight of Waiting

Waiting feels safe — but it's the kind of safety that suffocates you.

The longer you wait, the heavier your un-lived life becomes. Dreams don't stay light forever; they gather weight like stones in your pocket until carrying them exhausts you.

I've watched people spend their best years circling the edge of what they wanted — waiting for certainty that never arrived.
They grew older, more cautious, more hesitant — and one day they looked back and realized they had waited themselves into regret.

Opportunities rarely announce themselves.
They appear *while you're moving*, not while you're standing still.

True Hard Fact:

Motion attracts opportunity. Hesitation repels it.

Imperfect Beginnings

Every great story you admire began in imperfection.

Michael Dell didn't start in a corporate office — he started in a dorm room, building computers by hand.
Ralph Lauren didn't begin in department stores — he began selling ties out of his car trunk.
Colonel Sanders didn't open his first restaurant with investors — he was living out of his car, knocking on doors, asking people to taste his recipe.

None of these beginnings looked impressive.
Most looked foolish at the time. But they were *beginnings*.

And beginnings — even shaky, awkward ones — carry more power than perfect plans that never leave the page.

True Hard Fact:

The smallest start beats the biggest intention.

You don't need every detail figured out.
You don't need to feel ready.
You don't need approval.

You need the courage to start with what's already in your hands.

Momentum Is Born in Motion

Here's the paradox: **confidence doesn't create action — action creates confidence.**

A child doesn't learn balance by thinking about it. He learns by wobbling, falling, getting up again — until one day the fall turns into a stride.

Your life works the same way.
The moment you act, something shifts. You gain experience. You learn what doesn't work. You discover what might.

Little by little, courage builds.

Momentum doesn't come from perfect plans — it comes from movement.

True Hard Fact:

You don't find your footing before you move — you find it while you move.

The Cost of Delay

Waiting isn't harmless — it's expensive.
Every delay carries a price.

The door you hesitate to open today might not exist tomorrow.
The apology you postpone, the risk you avoid, the dream you delay — each has an expiration date.

Think of how many people have said, *"One day I'll..."* — and never did.
Books unwritten. Businesses unbuilt. Words unspoken.

Regret doesn't come from failure — it comes from never trying.

True Hard Fact:

You can recover from failure. You can't recover from never starting.

Start Now

So, let's make this plain: stop waiting.

Start where you are — with trembling knees, limited resources, and an uncertain plan.
Begin with the crooked, mismatched pieces already in your hands.

You may not know the ending. You may not even know the middle. But you will *never* discover what's possible until you begin.

Life doesn't reward those who wait for the perfect moment — it rewards those who begin in imperfection and grow along the way.

True Hard Fact:

Starting ugly beats waiting beautifully — every single time

Chapter 17 — Forget About Goals

The Problem with "GOALS"

Fact is: Most so-called "success experts" worship goals. They tell you to write them down, color-code them, and map out the next five, ten, or twenty years of your life.

It sounds smart — until you realize most goals fade like New Year's resolutions.
The excitement burns fast, then guilt sets in. What once inspired you now feels like a weight that you're dragging uphill.

Because what's supposed to move us forward often ends up paralyzing us. I have a different take. I believe the word **GOALS** really stands for:

Generating **O**verwhelming **A**nxiety **L**imiting **S**uccess.

And as the old Yiddish proverb reminds us: *"Mann tracht, un Gott lacht"—"Man plans, and God laughs."*

A Different Approach

So, here's a better way: stop worshiping distant finish lines and focus on what you can do *today*.

Make a list — not of grand achievements, but of meaningful actions. Some days the list will be long; some days it will be short. What matters is progress, not perfection.

You don't climb a mountain in one leap. You climb it one step, one breath, one small victory at a time.

True Hard Fact:

Direction matters more than distance.

Living in the Present

No amount of regret can rewrite the past.
No amount of worry can guarantee the future.

Tomorrow isn't promised, and yesterday is gone. The only time you have is now — this hour, this choice, this moment.

That's why it's called *the Present* -- and that isn't a coincidence -- it's a gift.

Open it. Use it. Don't waste it.

True Hard Fact:

You can't live yesterday again, and you can't live tomorrow early. You only have today.

The End-of-Day Ritual

At the close of each day, take inventory:

- Celebrate what you finished. Small victories stack up into major wins.
- Notice what remains undone. If it still matters, carry it forward — not with guilt, but with intention.

This simple ritual builds momentum. It replaces frustration with focus. It shifts your attention from perfection to progress.

And over time, that shift becomes life-changing.

True Hard Fact:

The person who moves a little every day will outdistance the one who waits for the perfect start.

Final Word

Forget the myth of perfect goals. Build a system that keeps you steady. Win today, then win tomorrow.

Because life doesn't reward the best planner — it rewards the one who keeps moving.

True Hard Fact:

Progress is built in inches, not leaps. And those inches belong to the one who starts now.

Chapter 18 — When Quitting Looks Easier

The Difference Maker

Fact is: If I could hand you one quality that almost guarantees success, it wouldn't be talent, wealth, or luck. It would be **persistence.**

Talent is useful, but it fades when life gets hard.
Wealth can open doors, but it can't carry you through storms.
Luck may help you start — but persistence is what keeps you walking after the door has been slammed in your face.

Persistence is the quiet strength to keep going when quitting looks easier.

True Hard Fact:

The strongest people aren't those who never fall — they're the ones who never stay down.

Why Persistence Matters

Life will test you. Every dream that matters will come with obstacles. The question isn't **if** you'll fall — it's **what** you'll do after you fall.

Most people quit too soon. They stop one step short of the breakthrough, underestimating how close they were to success.

The truth is, the line between failure and victory is razor thin — often just one more try, one more day, one more act of faith when everything in you wants to stop.

True Hard Fact:

You never know how close you are when you give up — and that's why you don't.

The Fine Line Between Persistence and Stubbornness

There's a difference between **persistence** and **stubbornness.**

Persistence holds tightly to the dream but adjusts the path when necessary.
Stubbornness clings to the path even when it's clearly wrong.

Persistence listens. It learns. It evolves.
Stubbornness closes its ears and calls it conviction.

True Hard Fact:

Persistence is wisdom with endurance; stubbornness is pride with blinders on.

Building Persistence

Persistence isn't something you're born with — it's something you build.

- **Set your eyes on the long game.** Stop expecting overnight success.
- **Break the mountain into steps.** One small victory at a time will carry you forward.
- **Use failure as fuel.** Every mistake holds a lesson — take it and move on.
- **Stay accountable.** Walk with people who won't let you quit when it gets hard.

Like a muscle, persistence grows stronger the more you use it.

True Hard Fact:

The habit of finishing is built long before the finish line.

Generational Endurance

When you persist, you don't just carry yourself — you carry everyone watching you.
Children, grandchildren, coworkers — they learn how to stand by watching you refuse to fall apart.

Your endurance becomes their inheritance.
Your example becomes their permission to keep fighting.

True Hard Fact:

Your persistence today becomes someone else's courage tomorrow.

Keep This in Mind

Success doesn't always belong to the smartest or the most gifted.
It belongs to the one who simply refuses to stop.

So, when quitting looks easier — **press on.**
Dig deeper. Take the next step.

Because the reward often waits just beyond the place where most people gave up.

True Hard Fact:

The finish line always belongs to those who keep going when others quit.

Chapter 19 — The Strength of Restraint

The Backbone of Character

Fact is: Self-discipline is the quiet strength that holds everything else together.
Without it, even the greatest dreams collapse.
With it, ordinary lives accomplish extraordinary things.

Discipline is not about punishment — it's about **direction.**
It's the daily choice to pursue the long-term good instead of the short-term desire.

True Hard Fact:

Discipline is the bridge between intention and integrity.

The Struggle We All Face

Every one of us fights the same internal battle: the war between what's easy and what's right.

It's easier to **spend** than to save.
Easier to **speak in anger** than to hold your tongue.
Easier to **quit** than to keep going.

But "easy" rarely leads to "strong."
The stronger road demands restraint.

True Hard Fact:

What costs you comfort today builds your character tomorrow.

The Cost of No Restraint

When discipline disappears, life starts to unravel.

Health breaks down when appetites go unchecked.
Finances collapse when spending outruns saving.
Relationships fracture when words outrun wisdom.

We like to blame circumstances, but most of our pain is self-inflicted — the result of unrestrained choices.

What feels like freedom in the moment often reveals itself later as bondage.

True Hard Fact:

The price of freedom is self-control — and it's due every day.

Guardrails for Life

Think of discipline as guardrails on a mountain road.
They aren't there to steal your freedom — they're there to save your life.

Without them, every turn becomes dangerous.
With them, you can drive with confidence, knowing your path is protected.

Discipline works the same way. It creates boundaries that protect your health, your integrity, and your future.

True Hard Fact:

Boundaries don't limit your freedom — they preserve it.

Seasons of Discipline

- **In youth**, discipline builds foundation. It forms habits that will carry you for decades.
- **In the middle years**, discipline provides steadiness. Responsibilities are heavy, and distractions multiply. Discipline keeps you on course.

- **In older years**, discipline becomes legacy. It lives in the example of your consistency and the peace of a well-ordered life.

At every stage, restraint is strength.

Freedom Through Discipline

Some may think of discipline as chains — but the truth is the opposite.

The undisciplined are slaves to impulse: ruled by appetite, anger, fear, or laziness.
The disciplined deny themselves in the moment — and walk free.

They are not controlled by their feelings. They are guided by their purpose.

Restraint is what makes real freedom possible.

True Hard Fact:

If you can't say "no" to yourself, someone else will control you for you.

Building Discipline

Discipline isn't built in one heroic act. It's built one decision at a time. And strength in one area spills into another:
Learning restraint with money builds patience.
Practicing restraint in speech builds humility.
Controlling your time builds clarity and peace.

Each decision compounds — quietly building the backbone of your life.

True Hard Fact:

You don't build discipline once — you build it daily.

Chapter 20 — Waiting Without Losing Heart

The Test of Time

Fact is: Patience is one of the hardest virtues to master.
We live in an age of speed — quick answers, instant gratification, everything now.

But the deepest things in life can't be rushed.
Growth takes time.
Healing takes time.
Wisdom takes time.

Impatience may give you a moment's relief, but it robs you of lasting strength.
Patience trains the soul to endure the process so that when the time is right, the reward is real.

True Hard Fact:

Anything that grows fast usually dies fast. The strong things take time.

Why Patience Matters

Impatience leads to foolish choices.
It makes you force outcomes before foundations are ready.
It strains relationships, ruins opportunities, and leaves you restless — even when you get what you wanted.

Patience, on the other hand, teaches **trust.**
It slows your breathing.
It clears your mind.
It steadies you when life feels unfair or slow.

Delay is not always denial. Sometimes it's preparation.

True Hard Fact:

Impatience builds regret. Patience builds results.

The Slow Work of Growth

Think of a seed buried in the soil. It disappears from sight, but that doesn't mean nothing is happening.
Beneath the surface, roots are spreading. Strength is being built in secret before life breaks through the ground.

Patience works the same way. Much of what's growing in you right now is invisible — and that's how it should be.
Because the deeper the roots, the stronger the life that follows.

True Hard Fact:

Just because you can't see progress doesn't mean it isn't happening.

The Discipline of Restraint

Patience isn't passive — it's **active restraint.**
It's the decision to stay steady, keep working, and keep believing even when the results aren't visible.

It's the strength to hold the line when fear, pride, or frustration tempt you to act too soon.

True patience isn't weak; it's controlled power.

True Hard Fact:

Patience isn't waiting for the storm to pass — it's learning to work in the rain.

When Patience Is Tested

The hardest kind of patience isn't with time — it's with people.

Broken promises, careless words, repeated flaws — these will test your spirit.
But patience with others is often the truest measure of love.

Patience is also tested in the long seasons — waiting for an answer, a door to open, or healing to come.
Those are the moments when patience stops being a nice idea and becomes the truest measure of character.

True Hard Fact:

Patience doesn't mean you stop caring. It means you stop controlling.

Keep This in Mind

Patience doesn't weaken you — it refines you.
It gives you the strength to endure, the humility to learn, and the wisdom to wait for what's real.

Because the timing of life isn't always yours to control — but how you wait always is.

True Hard Fact:

What you do while you wait determines who you become when it's over.

Chapter 21 - Standing Firm When Fear Calls Your Name

The Call of Fear

Fact is: Fear is a voice every person hears.
Sometimes it whispers. Sometimes it shouts.

It tells you to stay safe. To stay small. To step back from the edge. And while some fear protects you from real danger, most fear doesn't protect — it *prevents*.

Fear is a thief. It steals opportunity, silences your voice, and keeps you from the life you were meant to live.

Courage isn't the absence of fear — it's the decision to stand firm when fear calls your name.

True Hard Fact:

Fear's job is to stop you. Your job is to move anyway.

The Battle Within

The greatest battles of courage aren't fought on public stages — they're fought in silence, deep inside your own heart.

The fear of failure.
The fear of rejection.
The fear of loss.

These quiet fears rarely shout, but they work steadily, shrinking your world one hesitation at a time.

Courage begins the moment you decide that fear will not be the one to set your limits.

True Hard Fact:

Fear whispers "what if." Courage answers "even if."

What Courage Really Is

Courage is not recklessness. It's not blind action or careless risk.

True courage is **measured restraint** — the strength to move forward *despite* fear because the purpose is greater than your comfort.

It's speaking when silence feels safer.
It's standing when sitting down would be easier.
It's moving forward even when your knees are shaking.

True Hard Fact:

Courage doesn't erase fear — it commands it to follow, not lead.

The Cost of Fear, the Reward of Courage

Fear always takes more than it gives.
It robs you of moments that never return — opportunities missed, relationships avoided, victories never known.

Courage, on the other hand, pays you back with interest.
It may cost you comfort, ease, or pride — but it gives back strength, confidence, and peace.

The more you act with courage, the less fear controls your story.

True Hard Fact:

Fear leaves regret. Courage leaves legacy.

Courage in Daily Life

Courage isn't reserved for battlefields or bright lights.
It's needed in kitchens, offices, classrooms, and quiet rooms.

- **Courage is telling facts** when lying would be easier.
- **Courage is apologizing** when pride tells you to defend yourself.
- **Courage is changing direction** when staying the same feels safer.

These choices won't make headlines, but they'll build a life worth remembering.

True Hard Fact:

Real courage doesn't shout — it shows up.

Courage That Strengthens Others

Each time you choose courage, fear loses some of its grip.
The next decision feels easier. The next risk feels smaller.

Courage compounds — like strength earned through use. And courage is contagious. When others see you stand firm, something inside them rises too. Your courage may be the spark that ignites someone else's bravery.

True Hard Fact:

Your courage is permission for others to find their own.

Keep This in Mind

Fear calls every name. It never stops.
But so does courage — if you learn to listen.

When fear says *"You can't,"* courage whispers back, *"Watch me."*

Chapter 22 — The Crossroads of Life

The Power of Decisions

Fact is: Every decision, large or small, bends your path in one direction or another.
Some choices shout their importance. Others seem harmless, but echo for decades.

At every crossroads, your choices are shaping the person you're becoming — step by step, decision by decision.

True Hard Fact:

Life is not shaped by chance — it's shaped by the choices you make.

The Illusion of No Choice

Many people claim they "had no choice."
But that's almost never a fact.

Even when circumstances are beyond your control, you still choose your response.

You choose your attitude when life is unfair.
You choose honesty when lies would be easier.
You choose perseverance when quitting tempts you.

To deny your power of choice is to surrender your freedom.

True Hard Fact:

You can't always control what happens to you — but you always control what happens in you.

The Weight of Small Choices

The big decisions may headline your life, but it's the small, repeated ones that write the story.

- What you eat and drink.
- How you spend your time.
- The words you speak in passing.
- The thoughts you allow to take root.

These daily decisions, stacked quietly over time, shape your character more than any single grand moment ever could.

True Hard Fact:

Your habits are just your choices on repeat.

Choosing Well Under Pressure

The hardest choices are not made in silence — they're made under pressure.

When others are watching.
When compromise offers relief.
When standing firm comes with a cost.

That's where your true self is revealed.
It's easy to do right when it costs nothing.
Character shows when the right choice costs you something real.

True Hard Fact:

Pressure doesn't build character — it exposes it.

The Legacy of Your Choices

Every decision leaves a mark. Some fade quickly. Others last a lifetime.

Your choices ripple outward — into your family, your friendships, your work, and into generations you may never meet.

You can't control every outcome, but you can control the integrity of your decisions.
And those decisions, stacked one upon another, form the legacy you leave behind.

True Hard Fact:

Your choices are writing your legacy in real time — make sure the story is worth reading.

Keep This in Mind

Life won't always give you easy paths. But it will always give you crossroads.

When you reach one, don't rush.
Pause.
Look both ways — not just at what's convenient, but at what's right.

Because every choice matters — and one day, they'll tell the story of who you truly were.

True Hard Fact:

Your destiny isn't written by fate — it's written by the decisions you make when no one's watching.

A Final Thought… At Least for Now

If you and I were sitting together right now, maybe over a cup of coffee or walking side by side on a quiet path, this is what I'd tell you.

We've covered a lot of ground in these pages, but I know there are still questions out there—some I didn't touch, some I couldn't. And that's alright. No book, no teacher, no single voice has every answer. Life is too big for that. What matters is that you keep searching, keep learning, and keep listening to the whispers that guide you.

Along the way, you might stumble across books that have inspired millions before you—classics like *Think and Grow Rich*, *The Secret*, or *The Power of Positive Thinking*. You might also be drawn to the deeper wells of wisdom found in sacred texts: the poetry of the *Tao Te Ching*, the strength of the *Bible*, the clarity of the *Bhagavad Gita*, the devotion of the *Guru Granth Sahib*, or the meditations of the *Upanishads*. Each carries a torch lit long ago, still burning for anyone willing to walk by its light.

But here's the fact that I really want to leave you with: your journey is your own. It doesn't matter how fast you go, how many books you've read, or how perfectly you think you've done it. What matters is that you keep moving toward the life that feels honest and alive for you.

You're only old when regrets weigh heavier than dreams. And your journey only ends when your dreams do. So, keep dreaming. Keep reaching. Keep walking. The story isn't over—not yet.

K. D. Wood

Version Notes

Compiled and formatted January 2026

Final Author Layout – True Hard Facts by K. D. Wood

All text © 2026 K D Wood Legacy Books

All rights reserved.

Made in the USA
Coppell, TX
22 January 2026

69760561R10046